FOREVER *faithful*

FOREVER *faithful*

DEANE TALBERT

Tate Publishing & *Enterprises*

Published by Tate Publishing & Enterprises, LLC
127 E. Trade Center Terrace | Mustang, Oklahoma 73064 USA
1.888.361.9473 | www.tatepublishing.com

Tate Publishing is committed to excellence in the publishing industry. The company reflects the philosophy established by the founders, based on Psalm 68:11,
"The Lord gave the word and great was the company of those who published it."

Interior design by Chelsea Womble

Published in the United States of America

ISBN: 978-1-61566-073-5
1. Biography & Autobiography, Personal Memoirs
2. Religion, Christian Life, Inspirational
10.11.29

Dedication

To Rosalind and Bobby, Vern and Mary, my precious family

Table of Contents

Foreword

Use this book as an encouragement.

When Clifford and I were asked to take the pastorate positions of Abundant Harvest Worship Center in Memphis, Tennessee, we knew God had a purpose for us. We had never met Deane Talbert, but when we did meet, we knew that she was one of our reasons for being at the church. She is a very faithful saint and a very faithful friend to us. She is also faithful to the most important, God!

She is an inspiration to many in our congregation. In our three years as pastors, Deane has proven her faith and trust in God, who is the head of her life. We have seen several traumatic and devastating things happen to her, but these things have not wavered her faith in God.

In this book, you will read about her life as a child and all the struggles she went through. And then all the heartaches and disappointments she experienced in her marriage. But God has kept her, traveled with her for eighty-five years, and has proven his love for her. Now, she is still trusting him to let her live to see three more prayers answered before he takes her home to be with him.

I know you will enjoy every page of this book. So sit down, take the time, and be engulfed in reading the life story of one of the greatest ladies I have ever known.

—Carolyn Waldrop, pastor's wife
Abundant Harvest Worship Center

An Awesome Journey

Life is a great adventure,
If we only know the way
To let go and be happy
And live for each new day.
Just thank the Lord for the doors he opens,
To smile and help a neighbor
For the little things we do for others
Are acts of love—not labor.
As we fill our days with God's great love,
Each person becomes our friend,
Regardless of their attitudes;
Our days will happily end.
For as we give, we shall receive,
And God's blessings shall flow anew.
As we scatter sunshine along our way,
We will be enjoying it too!

—Deane Talbert

From Childhood to Marriage

From the age of five, I began searching for God and wondered if he really loved me. Mother would read the Bible to us sometimes and sing songs about God, especially "The Lily of the Valley." Sometimes Dad would sing "When the Roll is Called Up Yonder."

We attended church occasionally, for the church was miles away and we had to travel by buggy then, like everyone else. But I would wonder if there really was a God and if heaven was a real place.

When my brother Bill was born, I was over four years old. From then on I was no longer the baby and got very little attention. My sister, Mattie Elva, was nearly eight years older than me. She and Mother had a close relationship. They did the housework together, talking and laughing most of the time. When not working, they sewed or quilted together. I'd often ask if I could help, but they'd always tell me to get a book and read or go outside to play. I felt rejected.

My older brother, Sam, had always been in bad health, and Mother spent time doing things for him, even making tall glasses of eggnog mid-morning and mid-afternoon and during harvest time, taking it to him in the fields.

My younger brother was so affectionate he would jump in her lap often and hug and kiss her. Of course, she would hug and kiss him too. I'd watch them with longing but was too timid to be like him. I don't remember Mother ever kissing me, but I know she loved me.

Sometimes I'd pretend to be sick and stay in bed, complaining of sore throat or other pains to get her attention. She would always be worried about me then and spend lots of time with me, even cooking my favorite foods. She was a sweet Christian woman, and I'm sure she never realized that she made such a difference between the other children and me.

I remember when I was eight I was playing in the front yard with my brothers' ball when I accidentally threw it into a weed-grown vacant lot across the road. I was afraid I'd never find it. I prayed asking God, if he were real, to lead me to the ball. Then I walked into the tall weeds that came almost to my shoulders. Suddenly, my foot hit the ball, and I knew God had answered my prayer.

Mother died of pneumonia when I was fifteen, and Dad remarried six months later. He changed from a loving father to a man obsessed with trying to please his new wife. She had two children, a girl a year younger than me and a son two years older.

My dad was a prosperous farmer and had a good bank account. She bought a new wardrobe of lovely clothes for her daughter and taught her to drive the new car my dad had just bought. I asked her to teach me to drive too, but she said that her daughter and she were all the chauffeurs the family needed. She also took charge of the finances, and my dad was afraid to buy me any new clothes or give me any spending money.

My sister got a full-time job and bought material to make my dresses. She worked as a salesclerk six days a week and did our laundry at night on a rub board, for we didn't have electricity in the country then. She also sewed at night, making lovely dresses for me, for she was a great seamstress!

My stepmother had me do dirty chores but

never asked her daughter to, not even do dishes, which I had to do every day. I couldn't bring girlfriends home to spend the night, but her daughter did often.

Almost a year after Mother died, I was on a double date when the boys decided to buy four half-pints of whiskey from a dealer on the riverfront. It was illegal to sell liquor in Arkansas then. They gave my girlfriend and me a bottle; then they started to drink. I wanted to be like them, so I raised the bottle to my lips. Before I could drink, I heard my mother's voice saying, "Deane, I've taught you better than that." I was shocked, for I knew she was in heaven, and God was warning me through her. I gave my bottle to my date and said, "You guys share this; I'd rather have a coke." They did and I got my coke. This was more evidence that God loved me!

Since we didn't have electricity, we had to use flat irons, heating them on the cookstove. One day as I was doing the ironing for my sister, brother, and myself, my stepmom kept moving the irons to the back of the stove so they couldn't heat. Finally I asked her to stop, but she only smiled and kept moving them. In desperation, I went to Sis, busy in our room, and told her. She went to the kitchen and confronted our stepmom. Our stepmom went to her and Dad's room and came back with a pistol, aiming it at my sister.

God gave me the courage to disobey Dad and stand up to her, for Dad had told me to never come against her, no matter what she said or did. He said his marriage came first and we had to please her. I yelled at her, "If you kill my sister, you will be sorry, for I'll see to it that you will pay over and over and over again." She looked at me then put the gun away. She never told my dad, and neither did I, for he would have taken up for her.

He was so in bondage to her that even at Christmas or birthdays he was afraid to do anything for us. But her children got anything they wanted. I've always been grateful that God brought us safely through it all but began to hate my dad and had to ask God to help me forgive him years later.

My older brother married soon after Dad remarried, and Sis married during my senior year in high school. Then my stepmom became even crueler to me. I was thinking of running away when Sis heard how I was being mistreated and left her husband to come home to help me. Her husband divorced her soon afterward. After seeing how I was being treated and Dad just ignoring everything, Sis tried to talk to him, but he only became angry with her.

One day at breakfast I told Sis I wasn't going to school that day. She asked if I was sick, but I said no. Then she asked if I had a test; again I said no. I then told her I didn't know why but felt I should stay home that day. She said no more.

About ten o'clock Dad came to our room, which he seldom did. Sis was glad to see him and greeted him joyfully. Suddenly, he threw her to the floor and started beating her unmercifully. I tried to pull him off her but couldn't.

I grabbed a broom, ran to the front porch, and started shouting for our neighbor across the road to help us. Dad came out and tried to pull me inside, but I resisted, saying, "If you want to beat me too, do it on the porch where the neighbors can see you." That calmed him and he left.

Sis and I knew that was the reason I couldn't go to school. God had kept me home to save her life. I've always thanked God for obeying his prompting. Dad thought she would ruin his marriage by protecting me.

Sis moved Bill and me to an empty tenant house on Dad's farm. She sent us to school and took complete charge of us. She really worked hard trying to give us a good life.

One day as I sat on the steps watching Sis at work in our garden, I began thinking what a sacrifice she was making to take Mother's place for Bill and me. God started giving me a poem for her. I got paper and began writing the words. Later I read it to her, and she really appreciated it.

To a Tranquil Lady

(My Ever-loyal Sister)

You have more patience than a bee that
Works all day, and yet can't see a day's rest
In the future.
You take rebuffs then turn your cheek
And look away as if to meet the next
One still more calmly!
Why do you stay at home and wait and fill the
Other fellow's plate, instead of deciding your
Own fate and striving to mold it?
Is it because your lingering grief numbs
Your energy and makes you weak
Against clamoring duty?

For everyone whom God lets live,
Someplace in life he will surely give
That they can fill very satisfactorily.
And this much I know, though you may scoff,
The finer things which you're made of
Weren't made to dwell so humbly.

My sister, brother, and I had been attending a little country church for some time when an evangelist held a revival there. He really convinced me that I needed to make Jesus Lord of my life. I accepted him as my Savior and will never forget how everything seemed so beautiful the next day.

I was baptized along with several others that weekend. The baptismal service was held at a creek several miles away. I'll never forget the great experience I had as I was walking toward the creek to be immersed in the water.

It seemed a multitude of angels was just above me, singing the most beautiful song I'd ever heard. Their voices blended perfectly, and the melody was one I'd never heard before; neither had I heard such glorious voices! The Lord didn't open my spiritual eyes to see them then. But many years later, he brought them to me again, and I saw them as well as heard them. They were clothed in lovely pastel gowns. The second time they were singing a familiar song of praise.

I knew the day I was baptized that I'd heard an angel choir, and God was letting me know he was pleased at the step I was taking toward him.

I had always wanted to be a nurse. When I learned the hospital in Blytheville didn't charge an entrance fee as the larger ones in Memphis did, I persuaded Sis to help me enter for training. We had to have three white uniforms, white shoes, and two pairs of white hose. Sis got them for me.

The hospital was very short of help, and I was the only new probationer. The other nurses took advantage of that and had me do all the chores requiring heavy lifting and intensive cleaning. We were on duty for twelve hours each day, seven days a week. We had a class once a month after work, taught by a doctor.

There were two patients in body casts. One was a very large lady and the other an elderly man. I had to change their bed linens and lift them for other reasons several times a day. I had complete charge of a man with scarlet fever as well, for the other nurses were afraid to enter his room. I had to wash my hands in Lysol water each time I entered his room and scrub his room with Lysol too.

Sometimes I'd have to stop and pray for God to give me strength and the right attitude about everything to keep on the job and maintain peace of mind. I was the only nurse who attended church and could only go on Sunday night after work.

After several months, I became ill with malaria fever and had two severe congestive chills. During the second attack, they had to pack my entire body in ice bags. They called my family, for I almost died. Only my sister came to see me.

The doctor said if I had another such attack I couldn't live, so I had to give up my dream of being a nurse. I had lost a lot of weight and weakened my health.

Circumstances were no better at home, so Sis and I decided to move to Memphis and get an apartment and jobs there. Our stepmom was so glad we were leaving that she didn't mind Bill living with her and Dad.

Our neighbors' sister and husband were visiting them and offered us a ride with them back to Memphis where they lived. We could only take a few boxes of our most treasured items, some clothing, and a box of home-canned vegetables. We had faith that we would find jobs. I had walked to town and sold our chickens for enough to last us a couple of weeks.

This was during the depression in 1938, and jobs were hard to find. Sis found a job in a small café for three dollars a week, and I got a job in a small hotel as a receptionist for four dollars weekly. Our one-room efficiency apartment cost two dollars weekly, but we could buy a week's supply of food for two dollars, so we did okay.

Marriage and Family

The hotel owner where I worked was a single man. He started inviting me to dances and movies after I'd worked only a few days. I would thank him but always made excuses. He wouldn't give up, so I finally told him if he really wanted us to go places together, he needed to go to church with me.

He was surprised but agreed, so we attended church together on our first date. He seemed to enjoy the service and started going to church with me every Sunday. We started playing checkers and reading the Bible together after work hours. Finally I agreed to go to good family-type movies with him.

After we had dated for a few weeks, he asked me to marry him. He said he'd never met a girl like me who would rather go to church than dances, and he wanted me for his wife. He seemed so lonely and alone that I thought we'd have a good life together, so I agreed if he would wait until Christmas.

On December 2 we went to a Bing Crosby movie with another couple. The movie was *Paris In Springtime*. After the movie he wanted us to go to Hernando, Mississippi, and get married. He was so eager and excited that I relented and agreed. The other couple went with us, and we were married at one o'clock, December 3, 1938, by a Baptist pastor. His wife and our two friends were our witnesses.

Shortly after the wedding, I had a rude awakening. I'd never been around heavy drinkers before and had never seen a drunken person in my life, until I discovered my husband was an alcoholic. He had never drunk anything but cokes and coffee with me before we married. Now he started drinking beer and vodka in excess.

When his brother and his wife visited us, they all drank together and urged me to join them, but I wouldn't. His brother's wife told me that she never drank before she married then said I'd soon be drinking with them. I never did.

Even though my husband went regularly to church with me before we married, he claimed he knew as much as the preacher now and wouldn't attend. He insisted that I stop going to services, but I refused.

He wanted us to try the Christian Science church. There they taught God was just a state of mind and not a reality. I never went back. Then he wanted to try a Lutheran church. There they gave us a book. The congregation would read one sentence, and the pastor would read the next until we'd read a page. There was no singing or music, only the short reading and a prayer.

After that I started attending a nearby Baptist church, but he seldom went with me. The pastor wasn't very deep in the Bible and always preached a very lukewarm sermon, talking mostly about his hospital visits—not very inspirational! I wanted more from God, for he never taught deeper truths.

We'd been married about a year and a half when our first child, a son named Kenneth, was born. His dad loved him and spent time playing with him when he was sober.

When Ken was about two years old, he ran in front of his dad holding up his arms to be loved, and his dad grabbed him and gave him a hard spanking. He was on his way to buy more beer, already nearly intoxicated, and was angry for being hindered.

After I'd quieted Ken, I quickly packed a

few things for my son and me and called a cab. I asked the driver to take us to a little-known hotel, and he did. Then I called Sis and told her where we were and why. I asked her to not tell my husband where we were.

The next day I saw a lawyer and started a divorce. I kept in touch with Sis, and she said my husband kept asking her about us and trying to find us.

One day as Ken and I were walking near the hotel, my husband drove by and stopped. He jumped out of the car, grabbed me, and begged me to come home. I told him he'd promised too many times to stop drinking, and I couldn't let him start hurting our son as he had before I left. He promised again he'd stop drinking, but I told him I'd already filed for a divorce. He begged for another chance to prove himself and promised, if I'd drop the divorce, he'd never drink again. I could tell he was really serious this time, so I went back home and stopped the divorce.

He kept his word and stopped drinking but became obsessed with becoming a millionaire. He did have a good mind for new ideas and could have become that millionaire he envisioned, if he could have followed through with some of his ideas. In fact, he had a blueprint engineer draw up plans for a city under one roof. This was really a drawing of the suburban malls that are so common today. This was in the early forties before any malls were built, so the engineer must have used my husband's plans for himself.

Since he wasn't financially able to build the mall, he started buying up old homes, always large ones, and converting them into efficiency apartments. This was before the apartment building boom. Sufficient housing was hard to find, so we always had plenty of tenants.

Within five years, he sold these converted houses and bought a nice two-story brick hotel in a good neighborhood. The owner was old and wanted to retire, so we bought it for a good price. It was beautiful with trees, shrubs, and a lovely rose garden on a large side lawn. It was a two-and-a-half-acre lot with a circular gravel driveway around the hotel.

By then we had another son and a small baby girl. Our lives could have been happy if my husband had not been so money conscious that all he thought of was more money. He became so miserly with the children and me that I had to scrimp on groceries and buy the children's clothing by the layaway plan, even their Christmas gifts and birthday presents. We had a good income, but though I did most of the work, he kept the money. I wanted to get a job so the children and I could have more, but he wanted me to take care of the hotel while he traveled or just left each morning to go wherever he wanted to go. When he learned I could type, he bought a typewriter and had me write letters to many different sources. He spent a lot on blueprints for different types of business projects but was never able to follow through.

When my younger son, Vernon, was about seven, one of the regular tenants' children kept annoying him as he was trying to play ball, until Vernon finally slapped him. The child ran and told his dad. The man came to the office and told us. Then Vernon's dad threw him on the floor and started beating him with a baseball bat. When I couldn't stop him, I went to the phone to call the police. That stopped the beating.

The next day Vernon and two friends went to the woods not far from the neighborhood. His friends came back and told me my son wasn't coming home but was staying overnight in a tree. The next morning he would be leaving, just following the Nonconnah River. I had a little money saved and gave it to them to go bring Vernon home and tell him to stay in a vacant room downstairs, that his dad would be okay and I loved him. My son never cared for his dad after that.

I never knew of the great love and power of our Lord until my older son had a near fatal accident while running a race with his brother. As he started to jump a wooden fence bordering the driveway, his foot caught in some wire lying beneath the fence. This caused him to fall face down on the gravel driveway. He was moaning in terrible pain, but his dad refused to let me call a doctor.

I did call and talk to the doctor, telling him how Ken fell, and he thought he'd only torn some tissue loose and sent a codeine prescription to the nearby drugstore. Ken tried to take the medicine but vomited blood. He couldn't eat or drink at all.

For three days he suffered, but when his kidneys stopped functioning, I called a cab and took him to the doctor, with his dad trying to stop me. The doctor said his appendix was about to rupture and wanted to take him to the hospital and operate at once. I said it wasn't his appendix and wanted a surgeon to check him first.

At the hospital a surgeon checked him then had X-rays made that showed his liver was torn to bits. He was given glucose and blood transfusions that night to strengthen him for surgery the next day.

After surgery, the doctor said he couldn't live more than twenty-four hours, for they had to remove the blood clots and most of his liver and sew him back up, that no one could live without a liver longer than twenty-four hours. I told him nothing was impossible with God, for him to do what he could and God would do the rest. It was amazing how the Holy Spirit began guiding me to faith scriptures and building my faith, though I'd read the Bible for years.

When the surgeon saw my faith, he started experimenting on Ken and told me he'd never seen anyone with the faith I had, that he'd do all he could to save him.

Ken was under an oxygen tent and taking IVs and medication for infection. All his veins collapsed, and he was taken to surgery to insert a needle above his ankle and tubes in his sides for IVs and to remove the bile since he had no liver to control it. The leg became infected from so many IVs, and the needle had to be removed.

He almost died several times and actually did die once. They didn't have ICU then but brought him to his room. After a few hours, nurses quit checking him, so I tried to awaken him but couldn't. About the twelfth hour after surgery, I checked his pulse, but he had none; then his heart, no response there. So I went to the nurse station and told them Ken was deceased. They ran to the room and saw he was dead.

Even though I'd never heard of anyone outside the Bible being raised from the dead, I prayed for God to give life back to Ken. I knew I had to promise God to begin taking him and his brother and sister to church and Sunday school regularly. When I made that commitment, God gave me back my son. The doctor later told me that he had died, and it was a miracle. He said he would write it up in the medical journal.

My husband got so upset over the huge hospital bills that he told the surgeon to get off the case and take Ken off the oxygen and other expensive medication. The doctor asked me if I wanted him off the case, and I told him to keep doing all he could, that we had a good income and I'd get a job and pay the bills if my husband didn't. He kept doing all he could and told my husband to find a prayer closet and start praying.

When Ken was finally healed after six months,

the surgeon said be should have been dead long enough to be shooting up daisies.

This made God very real and precious to me. I was hungry for a church where the pastor really knew God and preached under the anointing.

My Teaching Ministry Begins and Miracles Continue

The Sunday school superintendent had visited Ken at the hospital and saw the faith I had for his healing when it seemed impossible for him to live. He asked me to teach a class of eleven- and twelve-year-old girls, but I told him I'd never taken a course in teaching. He insisted I teach anyway, saying my faith and love of God was training enough. I started teaching against my husband's opposition, and God helped me make his power and love real to those little girls.

Those girls loved me and visited me often. I gave them prizes each quarter for good attendance and bringing visitors, and my class soon became the largest in the department. I loved to teach them, for they were eager to learn and growing spiritually.

About a year after Ken's healing, I became very ill with pneumonia and soon became so weak I had to stay in bed. When I told my husband, he refused to get a doctor, so I had to get breakfast, send the children to school, and take care of the hotel, for he would leave as soon as he ate breakfast. I stayed in bed when I could but had to get up often to rent apartments, collect rent, and answer the phone. I'd be so weak I had to hold on to the wall or chairs to walk, but God gave me strength to keep going. When the children were ill, I'd wait until he left, which he always did if one of us was sick, then take them to a nearby doctor's office, but I had to just trust God for myself.

One night, after a week's illness, Vernon came to my room and sat in a chair near my bed. After a while I told him he needed to get some sleep so he could go to school the next day. He told me that he didn't want to leave me, for if I died, he didn't want to live either. That nearly broke my heart, but I told him God would heal me and he needed some sleep. Finally I convinced him I'd be okay, and he left.

After the children left for school two days later, I lay down again. I was so weak I felt like I was sinking into a soft cloud. I knew I was dying and was glad, for I knew I'd soon be with Jesus. I felt such a peace until just as I was losing consciousness, God brought my children's faces before me. I knew they were in school, but there they were above my bed, looking down at me with such sad little faces.

I knew this was the Lord showing me how very much my children needed me. I then asked the Lord to let me live as long as the children needed me. Suddenly, I felt a great wave of strength flow through my body and knew the Lord was healing me! God is so faithful to meet our needs and never fails us.

Not long after I was healed, Vernon became very ill with a high fever and night sweats. I wanted to call the doctor, but his dad wouldn't let me. Vernon was too ill to walk to the doctor's office, so, after his dad left for the day, I called the doctor and told him how very sick my son was.

Dr. Johnson left his office and patients and hurried to the hotel. He still had his white medic coat on and had brought medicine for Vernon. He seemed to know what was wrong and gave him an antibiotic shot after checking him. Then he left medicine to heal him, saying he had strep throat. When he started to leave he stopped, turned back, and said to me, "If you ever need to divorce your husband, I'll be glad to be a good witness for you." He knew how money-mad my husband was and only charged me a fraction of his regular fee.

A few days later, when he was feeling much better, Vern told me he wanted to show me something. I stopped and watched him prop his knees up in the bed, pretend he had his air rifle, take careful aim, and *boom*! He then said he was going to kill his dad as soon as he was able. I told him he couldn't do that, but he said he was going to do just that. I had to hide his air rifle to prevent it.

Not long after this, his dad told Ken he had had enough school, so he had to quit and help with the hotel work. Ken was in the tenth grade and wanted to finish school but agreed to quit. I spoke up and said Ken would not give up his education and wasn't really needed at the hotel.

My husband became so angry he said he'd leave then. He began loading his car with clothes and other things but didn't leave. I kept sending Ken to school. Three days later he unpacked his car and said no more about Ken leaving school.

Though we had a good income, he fired the hotel maid and made me take over her work, as well as continue taking care of the hotel and all the home duties, including cooking and laundry.

I had so much hard cleaning in the apartments, where men and women had regular jobs, that I developed pleurisy in my lungs. The pain was so severe it was hard to do the work, but my husband insisted the work had to be done. Finally I became so ill I could hardly breathe. One of the tenants got a doctor for me. After X-rays the doctor said my left lung had collapsed. I had to have surgery to remove that lung.

My children wanted me to get a divorce, but when I prayed about it, I would feel I needed to stay, so I couldn't. I could only pray for my children and their dad and do all I could to help them have a normal life, having backyard picnics, playing games, and doing whatever I could for them.

My husband decided he'd stop me from attending church by writing the church board that my health was so bad that he was assuming all the responsibility for the business and family and that I could no longer attend church. He never meant what he wrote, for life went on as usual. I ignored the letter and kept going to church and taking the children.

I also kept teaching the Sunday school class. That enraged him, so he tried everything he could to stop me from serving God, even forbidding me to read the Bible. I quit reading it in his presence but never missed a day reading God's precious Word.

I invited one of our tenants to attend church with me one Sunday. She wasn't a Christian but had a huge goiter on her neck and was afraid of surgery. I told her that if she'd go to church and believe, God would heal her. As we were leaving, my husband stopped me and said, "If you go to church today, I won't be here when you return." She became frightened and said we'd better not go, but I told her to come, that everything would be fine. He never left and didn't try that approach again. She and her son started attending church after that. Her goiter was healed!

My husband started staying home more and became even greedier for money, hardly allowing me enough for adequate food for the family. I was careful to plan meals where we'd always have enough, but these were not the nutritious meals they needed.

I noticed the tenants weren't as friendly as usual and found my husband had told them that I was mentally ill and he was committing me to a mental hospital. He'd told them not to pay their rent to me any longer, but one long-time resident kept paying me until my husband demanded that he stop. When he refused, he was asked to move.

It is awesome how our Lord takes over when we are in deep need and have no answers. So often when a person tries to hurt someone, it boomerangs back to them. My husband began acting so weird I called his sister and asked her to come help me. She came and saw how strange he was acting. We took him to a psychiatrist who said that he was mentally ill but needed more treatment than he could give. We then had him checked by two others who said the same thing. One suggested that we enter him into the state mental hospital, so we did.

He was there four years and had extensive treatment. After being there three months, he was permitted to come home one weekend each month. I'd visit him by bus every two weeks, and his sister would take me to get him when he could come home.

These visits upset Vernon so much I made an appointment with the chief of staff at the hospital and told him how the visits were disturbing my teenage son. I asked to stop them. He said the man deserved a chance, but I told him my young son also deserved a chance for a decent life, that he wanted to quit school and his grades were being affected.

My husband came home once more, but God took over again. He checked the bookkeeping ledgers and saw how much I was paying on the huge debts he'd made, including the four mortgages, and saw how little was left for our living expenses. He broke down weeping for the first time over what he'd done and told me to take him back to the hospital and forget him, that he'd ruined our lives.

I felt great pity and forgiveness for him. I told him to turn to God, and we could work it out and have a good life together. He said he didn't deserve it and wasn't worth it. He never came home again.

Ken and I kept visiting him and taking books and Christian magazines, encouraging him to go to chapel and watch Christian television. Thank the Lord he did, and he is now in heaven and not crying out in hell!

A New Start

I got a small loan from my banker to make some much-needed repairs on the hotel. The tenants were very pleased about this. There was so much to do and so little cash after paying bills and debts that Ken wanted to drop out of school and help me, but I wanted him to finish school. He was in his senior year.

We compromised by him attending an accredited night school four nights a week. He saved over half the cost of labor by removing all the faded wallpaper, painting all the rooms, and making other repairs. He also graduated from high school.

I thought I was paying all the bills but didn't know taxes had not been paid for three years until I received a letter from the tax collector stating that since we'd not paid taxes for three years, we had two months to pay the three years' taxes. I couldn't possibly pay the full amount, for I'd been paying too many bills to save anything. I know my husband destroyed all the tax statements, for I never saw any.

This was in 1957, and inflation wasn't like it is now. The taxes were a little less than two thousand, and it would have been terrible to lose our property for so little. I tried to sell it, but no one wanted to go to court to settle the sale since my husband couldn't sign, being in a mental hospital.

After praying about it, I was led to take the threatening letter to a good lawyer. He had a lawyer friend who was interested in profitable real estate. When he looked over my property, he was interested but didn't want to pay the price I was asking. I was only asking $75,000 for both properties, which was very reasonable. They would sell for at least $350,000 now.

When he realized I wouldn't lower the price, he paid forty thousand for the four-apartment home with an option to buy the hotel in a year.

This was enough to pay all the bills, including the four mortgages and a failed car lot my husband had started. There was enough left to buy a nice three-bedroom home in west Memphis and a small business for my children and myself.

The children were so happy to have a nice

home at last and to be able to invite friends for dinner and weekends. We were only a few blocks from a good school that Vernon and Rosalind attended, and I was able to send Ken to college.

He was so thrilled to go to college but questioned me about affording the tuition. Tuition was very reasonable then, for it only cost five hundred dollars to enroll him in a good college in Missouri he wanted to attend. He worked the next three summers paying his expenses and graduated as an honor student.

The children made friends in the church and community, but neither Vernon nor Rosalind liked the public school. To finish their education, I sent them to a private school in Memphis. That too was reasonable, only forty dollars a month and not far from us. Vernon made good grades but soon got a job and started night school. He graduated and joined the navy, but Rosalind got married at sixteen before she finished school. I had wanted her to finish her education.

The lawyer bought the hotel. I had him pay monthly notes instead of cash, so I had a good income for nine years.

I'd wanted Rosalind to get a better education and have a good life, and I had tried so hard to help her, even letting her take a modeling course to be a model. She did well there and was told she'd make a good model, but she thought getting married was better.

Her husband was ten years older than her and came from a family who didn't believe Jesus was the son of God, only a good man who gave his life on a cross to help people. He agreed Rosalind could keep going to our church and went with her a few times. Then he told his brothers that he really liked our church and felt something when he was there. They told him it was a demon that he felt when it was only the Holy Spirit he was feeling. This scared him, and he stopped going.

After that his family began trying to turn Rosalind to their faith. She did go with them a few times, and a sister-in-law started visiting her once a week, bringing her Bible and trying to prove our King James Bible was wrong. If I'd not been praying fervently for God to show her the truth, she would have joined them, for she knew very little about the Lord even though I'd taken her to church regularly. She just wasn't interested then.

I visited Rosalind once when this woman was there, and she was very persuasive. But when she put another meaning on Scripture,

God helped me point out the truth with other scriptures. She soon gave up and left. She didn't continue the lessons, and Rosalind was convinced of the truth.

Her husband never went to church again and started drinking heavily and not paying bills. They had to move often, for he wouldn't pay the rent. After their first child was born, I helped a lot with their clothing and paid for a phone so Rosalind could keep in touch. I also loaned them the down payment for a car, and Rosalind got a job and paid me back while I babysat for her.

When Ken finished college, he was called to the ministry. After God had answered my fervent prayer in 1951 when he had the terrible accident that completely destroyed his liver, I knew that someday he would be called to preach the gospel, so this was truly God's leading for him.

Our pastor wanted him to be youth pastor of our church, for he was so good with teenagers. He had more than tripled youth attendance in our church and started a great youth ministry, but he told our pastor that God was calling him to be an evangelist.

The Lord used him in several states and old Mexico to lead people to know and love Jesus.

He had the faith to pray for many sick people, including children, and God would heal them.

After holding meetings in Texas and California, he was offered the position as pastor in both states, but he thanked them and turned down the offers.

My Move to California

In southern California Ken met a pastor that he really liked, and this man persuaded him to stay and work with him. Then he wanted me to come join him and started writing and calling me, saying I should come work with him and his new friend.

I didn't want to leave Memphis, for I was very active in my church as Sunday school teacher and president of the Women's Missionary Council. When he kept calling, insisting that I join them, I put out a fleece to the Lord that if I should go, then provide the extra money for the two-thousand-mile trip. I didn't expect it to be answered, but it was.

When I received the unexpected check for three hundred dollars, I knew I had to leave my hometown and join them. Ken was very glad to see me, and so were his friends. We rented a three-bedroom house at a very low price, and I started attending church services with them.

They were teaching on the ministry of

angels and the gifts of the Spirit. I had read the Bible through several times but had never heard sermons on these subjects. It made me hungry for the deeper things of God and to have these gifts in my own life.

I started spending most of the time reading the Bible and praying, and God began giving me the gifts of the Spirit. I was first baptized in the Holy Ghost and started speaking in tongues; then I received the gifts of interpreting messages in tongues and prophecy.

One morning as I was washing dishes, I looked out the window and saw a lovely, slender young woman running through the woods. She was wearing a lovely white dress with a white scarf around her shoulders, which was floating in the breeze as she ran. She was running gracefully down a narrow path singing a beautiful song. The Holy Spirit gave me the words to this song, and I quickly wrote them down.

Come Into My Kingdom

Won't you come into the kingdom now with me?
Walk the road of perfect love and purity.
As you take me by the hand and move upward through

the land
You'll discover precious jewels you now can't see.
Chorus:
Come into that kingdom now with me
Walk that road of perfect love and purity.
As you overcome each test, you'll come into the rest
I've prepared for those who love and honor me.
Before the inner door is opened to this land
You must yield your stubborn will to my command
Be ever helpful, loving, kind
Feed the hungry, heal the blind, this is my plan.
Won't you plunge into my kingdom now with me?
Break the shackles of this life and be set free.
You will bypass the grave and death
I will impart to you my wealth
As you enter Zion's hill and flow with me.

This happened on a bright, sunny morning with no woods in the neighborhood, so I knew God was opening my spiritual eyes and insight on how wonderful his kingdom is when we obey his Word and live for him. We must have love in our hearts for him and others before we can be a part of his precious kingdom. Jesus told his disciples that his kingdom was within and cannot be seen. In Romans 14:17 it is written, "The kingdom of God is not meat and drink, but righteousness and peace and joy in the Holy Ghost."

When Vernon finished high school, he joined the navy and was sent to a training camp in a very short time. When I went to California, he was already stationed at a naval hospital in Santa Anna, a town just sixty miles from Ken and me. He was able to spend some weekends with us, and it was good to have him and Ken together with me again.

A few months later, he was given a twenty-four-hour alert notice for service in Vietnam and got to stay with us until he left. During this time, I spent many hours praying for his safety in the war zone and kept seeking God's answer until I had perfect assurance that he'd not be wounded and would return safely.

I wouldn't listen to the news or read a newspaper, for I wanted to just trust God for his safety. I had asked the Lord to let me know when he was in danger. It was amazing how often he was in danger, and it was amazing how often God did just that! Sometimes he'd awaken me at night by hearing Vernon's voice calling "Mother" or just the word *Vernon* shouted. I'd always fall on my knees and pray for him until I would feel a peace come over me.

Once, he let me know Vernon was in great danger by hearing a song about the death march. I jumped out of bed and began rebuking death. Another time he showed me a vision of the naval hospital where Vernon worked as an X-ray technician swaying back and forth and almost collapsing, so I quickly reminded God of his promise to protect my son from danger. Then the large red brick building stopped swaying, and I knew the Lord had saved him again.

He had many narrow escapes, but God always protected him and brought him home a year later. It's so wonderful to just believe God's promises. When we truly trust God and stand on his promises, he never fails us.

Two Precious Visitations With Jesus

After Vernon left for the war zone, a dear friend of Ken's and mine, a woman evangelist named Juanita Leonard, and her husband, Bill, came to see me from another town. They took me out to dinner at a lovely high-class restaurant with palm trees and beautiful half-circle booths.

They were seated facing each other at each end of the booth, and I was in the center. As I looked at them gazing lovingly at each other, I said silently to God, "God, they are so happy, and I am so alone." Then I looked across the large restaurant and saw a beautiful, tall, slender man dressed in a long white robe coming toward me. He came directly to our booth, crossed the top of the long table, and sat down beside me. I knew it was Jesus and felt such a love and peace envelop me that I've never felt alone again.

Ken and Brother Cash went on a week's evangelistic trip to Arizona. One morning that week

I woke up and saw a mist like dew that started at the foot of the bed and completely covered me. I heard beautiful singing and looked toward my closed bedroom door. Above the door, on the ceiling, was a multitude of angels dressed in lovely gowns of many pastel colors of blue, pink, green, yellow, orchid, and white. They were singing a beautiful song of praise to our Lord!

I know I was alone, yet God's messengers of peace and beauty surrounded me. I was being blessed by the angel chorus. It was a wonderful experience I'll always remember.

Ken began working weekdays in San Bernardino, and I had a lot of time to read God's Word and seek his presence in prayer. One day as I was meditating on the scripture in Hebrews 10:22, which says, "Let us draw near with a true heart in full assurance of faith, having our hearts sprinkled from an evil conscience, and our bodies washed with pure water," I asked the Lord to reveal that to me, and he did.

The morning was chilly, and I was standing in front of an open gas heater that I had turned on for warmth. Suddenly, I saw a lovely waterfall cascading down from the wall behind and over the heater and stopping at my feet. I asked the Lord to cleanse me with his pure water and walked into the waterfall. I felt my legs burning, for I'd hit the heater, now invisible, and burned my legs.

I reached down and touched each burning leg, saying, "Jesus, heal them." He did, not even leaving a scar. I stayed under the waterfall until I felt completely cleansed and at peace. Then I walked to the couch in front of a large picture window.

When I looked out the window, I saw a cross on a hill not far away. Jesus was hanging on the cross with his head down. Blood was flowing from the large thorns in the crown on his head, and larger streams of blood were flowing from the nails in his hands. I dropped to my knees beside the couch and began crying out to God, asking why he was letting Jesus suffer so much. I began weeping in grief for Jesus. While still weeping, I saw myself standing a few feet behind me looking down at me, weeping for Jesus. Until then I had never believed in an out-of-body experience, but now I too had had one.

When I stopped weeping, I arose and looked at the cross on the hill again. Then I started walking toward it. When I stood before the cross, I looked up at Jesus and said, "Jesus, cover me with your blood." I stepped into the pool of blood on my left. Then I saw blood slowly covering my feet and coming up my legs, then my entire body. When my head was covered, I saw it swirl in a circle and stop. I felt completely washed from an evil conscience!

Then I was back before my couch and saw Jesus in an oval cloud beside my window. He was dressed in a long white robe. I looked at him and said, "Lord, raise me to resurrected life." I dropped to my knees before him. He stepped down from the cloud and took my hands, raising me up to stand beside him.

We started walking together, side by side, across the long living room. It was so wonderful and awesome to be walking with my precious Lord.

Someone started knocking very loud at the front door and Jesus disappeared, but I'll never forget this blessed spiritual experience.

This happened at about ten o'clock one morning, and only God knows how long it lasted. For me, time stood still.

Rosalind Needs Help, Vern's Miracle

While Vernon was in Vietnam, Sis began writing me about the difficulties Rosalind was going through. She had two small boys under three years old, and her husband was drinking more and not providing for the family. She wanted me to come back home to care for them.

I wanted to help my daughter and her two little sons, but when I prayed about it, I felt I could not. Once when I was praying, I saw myself on a cross and knew I had to look to the Lord for help for her. Finally I was given the peace to visit Memphis and see how they were, but only for a few days.

They were living in a small mobile home, and she had to do her laundry, even the bed linens and her husband's work clothes, in the bath tub. The toilet was stopped up, and a mother dog and her puppies were in a box in the living room. I saw maggots crawling on the floor near the box where the dogs were.

Rosalind couldn't care for her small sons properly with no plumbing for the toilet and while doing all the family chores without help or sanitation. I had to stay with Sis while there and couldn't be with Rosalind as much as I wanted to. It was hard to leave her and go back to California, but I had to.

Not long after returning to California, I had a word of wisdom from the Lord. It was a scripture he quickened to me that said, "Free them from the bondage and danger they are in." I called Sis, for Rosalind didn't have a phone, and asked her to tell my daughter I was sending a plane ticket for her and the boys to come to me. I sent the ticket, and soon she and the children were with me again. It was great to have them with me and to help with the little boys.

She was expecting her third child and was only twenty years old. She really had to grow up the hard way! She didn't want me to pay for a doctor for her and the baby, so she went to welfare for help. I felt so sorry for her, but I admired her determination to make her own way.

Her husband kept trying to get her to come back, but when she wouldn't, he came to

California and stayed with us. He finally got a job and helped with the groceries but not with a doctor for their expected child. This caused Rosalind to worry a lot, for she was afraid they would check on her, find out her husband was with her, and refuse to help.

We were having church services in the large living room and dining room area of our house, and many people from three nearby towns were attending. Sometimes the place would be filled with people standing around the walls, as well as having several rows of folding chairs and the two couches and chairs filled.

Ken's pastor friend, Paul Cash, had tried for over twenty years to organize a Bible school and missionary outreach but couldn't get it completed until Ken came. Ken was very good at organizing Christian outreaches and had organized a Christian club in college and youth ministry at our church. It only took Ken two weeks to make a suitable outline and draw up plans for the Bible school and missionary project.

Ken took these plans to the governor of California and got his seal of approval for them.

He named the project "Newness of Life" from the book of Romans, chapter six.

Even though Brother Cash preached some good truths that were helpful, he also taught some error, and the Lord let me know the difference. For example, he taught that we were already manifested sons of God and were not to associate with those not on our spiritual level. He didn't think we should have phones so the ones not on our level of spirituality could not reach us and waste our time with their problems.

I really wanted a phone, and Vernon told me later that if we'd had a phone he could have called me free from Vietnam, for he'd been made an officer in the navy and was privileged to call his family in the states. It really saddened me to know that, for I could have encouraged him.

Ken was such an admirer of Paul Cash that he thought anything he said or did was from God and couldn't grasp his false distortion of Bible scriptures. Brother Cash's excuse for not helping or caring for anyone outside our special group was that they were of the wrong spirit.

Jesus said we are to help anyone in need and to love our neighbors as ourselves. He also said to be no respecter of persons but to treat others as we wanted them to treat us.

Brother Cash kept saying God was going to destroy that part of California with an earthquake and that we needed to move to another state soon. We did have a small earthquake that rattled the dishes and broke a few objects that fell from shelves or walls. It hit harder near Los Angeles and separated a four-lane highway, causing two cars to fall into a lake.

This helped Brother Cash convince us that we needed to relocate. He then had us pray where to move and said God told him it was Boise, Idaho. He then told us the property we would buy in Boise would be for the church group, and we'd all own it together. By then he had limited our church group to just six families who would move to Boise.

We had formed a board. He was the president, I was the vice president, Ken was the administrator, and Brother Cash's daughter, Claire, was the secretary. Helen, the school teacher, Ken and I, three other families, and the Cash family were to start the church in Boise. He found an eighty-acre ranch with a large two-story house that we used for a church until a chapel was built.

Vernon married Claire a few months after returning from Vietnam. Ken married a sweet girl named Esther. She was lovely and had a loving and caring personality. Claire was attractive too but was so self-centered and spoiled that I was worried about their marriage. I knew it would not be easy for Vernon and that she would have her way and really be the head of the family. I was so right, for she was.

Back To Memphis

Rosalind's husband wanted to move back to Memphis, where his mom and brothers were. He asked me to go with them and help with the new baby and two little boys. I knew Rosalind would need help, for it was over two thousand miles back, so I went with them. I had planned to return to Boise but never did except to visit my two sons.

We stayed with Sis in Memphis, for she was now the manager of the hotel I formerly owned, until Rosalind's husband and I could get jobs. I rented an efficiency apartment there, and Rosalind's husband rented an old house.

Vern found employment at a Boise hospital where he was promoted to director of his department with a good raise in salary. He helped enlarge the department and increased the value of it to the hospital. He bought a nice brick home for Claire and himself.

Ken got a job as an insurance adjuster in Idaho. Vern and Claire had a son, and Ken and

Esther had a baby daughter. When their daughter was ten days old, Esther's mother took Esther and the baby to live with her and Esther's grandmother. It nearly broke Ken's heart, but Esther's grandmother told Ken if he would send two hundred dollars a month for a year he could have his family back.

He got a job as substitute teacher in a high school teaching chemistry and sent the two hundred each month for a year. He said at times he made very little more than that and hardly had enough to live on, but he was thankful to be able to send the support each month. When he couldn't get his family as promised, he came back to Memphis and got a job as auditor at Holiday Inns.

We got a two-bedroom apartment together and started attending a good church. Ken loved the Lord but was very unhappy without his wife and daughter. I felt so sorry for him and Esther, for I knew they loved each other and could have been happy together if Brother Cash and her grandmother had not interfered, especially Brother Cash. Brother Cash never wanted Ken to marry in the first place. He wanted Ken to work only for him and do the work of his ministry. He practically made a slave of Ken by telling him he was responsible only to God and not to his family. Esther's grandmother, who was also a pastor and had her own church, felt the same way abut Esther. He took Ken's high standards from him and practically made a slave of him.

Rosalind started attending a good full gospel church near her, but her husband never went with her. His mother was very upset that Rosalind wouldn't accept her religion.

Her mother-in-law took her husband to a mental hospital to get Rosalind committed and take her children from her. I received a call from a nurse there asking if I had a daughter named Rosalind. When I said yes, she told me that her husband and his mother were there trying to get her committed. I told the nurse that all my daughter needed was a husband who would take better care of her and her children and provide for them. This kept them from committing her but didn't help matters very much.

Soon after that, Rosalind gave birth to their first daughter. They already had three sons, and she was only twenty-three years old! Her mother-in-law came to stay with them and help with the new baby, but her real reason was to take her son and grandsons home with her.

Rosalind overheard her talking to her husband, telling him Rosalind wasn't a fit wife, for she wasn't a part of the kingdom, their religious faith. Even though he never accepted his mother's faith or went to Kingdom Hall with her, he left his wife and new baby and went home with her.

Their oldest son, James Ray, wouldn't leave his mother alone with the baby only two weeks old, even though his dad and grandmother tried to persuade him to go. Rosalind was very glad to have him with her, but he couldn't provide the food and other things she needed, for he was only six years old. He was a comfort to her, and I loved him so much for staying with his mother and baby sister.

In desperation, Rosalind finally called me and let me know that her husband had left her and not provided food for her and James or milk for the baby. She was giving the baby Kool-Aid that didn't satisfy her hunger, and she cried a lot. All she and James had were biscuits and gravy and Kool-Aid and water.

She had called her mother-in-law and asked her to tell her husband to bring some milk for his baby daughter and food for James Ray, but the woman told her it wasn't any of her business and refused to help.

Ken and I had to give up our apartment and move in with them, for they had no one else to help them. The house was large enough for our furniture too. It had a very large living room and three large bedrooms.

We started attending the church that Rosalind was going to, and the little boys especially enjoyed the Sunday school. Eddy, her middle son, loved his Sunday school teacher and looked forward to each Sunday.

Ken still had hopes of reconciling with his family, so he left for Idaho after about a year with us. He bought a good supply of groceries and paid a month's rent before he left. He soon found a job and an apartment in Idaho but was unable to get his family back.

Rosalind's husband brought the little boys back and visited us a few times but never brought any groceries or gave money to help us. I had to apply for help for household expenses through the welfare agency. I couldn't get a job to meet our needs, as Rosalind was too brokenhearted to work or take care of the children.

Welfare was good to me and not only gave me a check each month for our rent, utilities, and other needs, but also sent a woman twice a week to help me in the home and take me wherever I needed to go shopping.

After about ten months, Ken wrote me to join him in Idaho. He had bought a house with three bedrooms, large enough for Rosalind, her children, and me. He had three tricycles for the boys and a small tot's bike for the baby, then two years old.

Our Move to Idaho

I went to juvenile court and got permission from the judge to take the children to Idaho. A good friend offered to drive us there if I would buy the gas for the trip. She had a large station wagon, which was much better than the Greyhound bus I'd planned to use to move, and I could take much more than by bus. Rosalind decided to stay in Memphis and find a job. I hated to take the children without her.

It was a long trip to Arco, Idaho, not far from the Canadian border, but we only had to stop one night at a motel on the way. We had brought a lot of food, which helped with expenses. The children were good and played on a quilt in the back of her station wagon. Her teenage daughter helped a lot by playing with them and amusing them.

Ken was happy to see us and insisted that my friend, whom he knew and liked, stay overnight before going on to California, where she and her daughter had friends. But they wanted to finish their trip as soon as possible, so they visited for a while then left.

The children liked their new home and really enjoyed the tricycles Uncle Ken had given them. There were some neighbor children who came over often to play with them, so they were busy and happy. There was a nice children's playhouse in the backyard large enough for all of them to enjoy, and they played there a lot.

Idaho was Mormon country, so there were no full gospel churches there, only Mormon, Catholic, Baptist, and Church of Christ. Each Sunday morning, we had a worship service in our home. Ken would tell a Bible story that the children could understand and enjoy; then he would teach them a good short chorus. They especially enjoyed "How Big is God," "Jesus Loves Me," and "Deep and Wide."

Each Sunday one of them would volunteer to sing a solo of their favorite chorus. Donny, who was three but couldn't talk, started singing along with everyone else and was soon talking fluently! We do indeed serve a big God! Donny's favorite song was "Jesus Loves Me." He was soon singing it solo. Eddy told Ken that he liked his church better than the one in Memphis!

A local Pentecostal woman soon met Ken,

and she and her family started attending our services. She wanted to rent an empty building for Ken and her to start church, with them taking turns preaching. Ken felt that she couldn't be trusted and rejected her plan.

I kept in touch with Sis and Rosalind. She couldn't find a good job and was staying with Sis. After several months, Ken went back to Memphis and brought her to Idaho to live with us. He started a small real estate company that he named Integrity but had difficulty completing a sale, for a large Mormon company kept track of all his clients. He lost several sales by them contacting his clients and telling them that Ken was a greenhorn and didn't know good Idaho property, then selling them one of their listings.

Ken knew this woman who wanted to get a church for them needed more land for her big herd of cattle. He showed her some good property with a large lake on it. She liked it but went to the owner. She tried to get him to cut Ken out and sell directly to her, minus Ken's fee. This man refused to cheat Ken from the sale and told him what she had tried to do. This confirmed Ken's first discernment of her un-Christ-like character.

Several times clients would give earnest money down on a sale then ask for it back after being contacted by the Mormon company. This made it hard on us financially, but I was proud of Ken for being so compassionate. He was living up to his company's name of Integrity. And God always provided for us.

James and Eddy did well in school and liked their teachers. Ken became friends with the school principal, and he and his wife visited us several times. The first time they came, James and Eddy thought they had done something wrong and hid so they wouldn't have to face them. When they realized it was just a friendly visit, they came out and enjoyed seeing them.

They rode the school bus each day, and Eddy got a nice children's book for perfect attendance. We had heavy snows all winter, and the temperature got as low as 35 degrees below freezing. But Idaho is a dry climate, and we all stayed healthy; the roads stayed safe.

Without my knowing it, Ken made arrangements with a Christian home for children in Boise, Idaho, then told Rosalind and me about it. He said he was taking the children there the next week. Rosalind and I were very upset over this but could do nothing since he had been providing for all of us.

Rosalind got a room in Boise, and Ken paid the first month's rent and bought a good supply of groceries for her. She would go to see the children often and got help from Social Services so she could prepare for them and get an apartment.

She loved her children so much and had been through a lot for them, but Ken felt it was time to think of himself and try once again to get his own family back. He never did, for Esther did not know of her grandmother's promise to him and that he'd paid child support to her grandmother. I told Esther after the woman died.

Another Change and New Job

Sis had been writing me to come live with her, for her daughter Jane had married and moved out. She didn't want to live in her big house alone. I went back to Memphis to be with her after the children, Rosalind, and Ken left. In a short time I got a job at a Seven-Eleven store near Sis. I worked there until they sold it almost a year later.

I had always liked Lowenstein's department store and wanted to work there. I prayed about it then applied for employment. God answered my prayer in a wonderful way. After filling out an application, the woman there asked me to wait a short time and she'd be back. She soon returned with the buyer of women's name brand sportswear, and I was hired instantly and went to work the next day as head of the sportswear department! God is good!

I enjoyed working there and found favor with the management. I was very surprised when the owner of the store, Mr. Lowenstein himself, came from his office to interview me. He asked how I liked the merchandise and how the sales were going, and he was pleased when I gave him a good report.

One of the salesclerks in the next department of regular ladies' wear was very hurt that she didn't get my job, for she told me that she had been working there for thirty years and had never gotten a promotion or raise in salary. I felt very sorry for her and tried to be a good friend and encourage her.

When I learned that no one ever got a raise there and that there were very few benefits, no sick leave, and only five holidays a year, including Christmas, I decided to take the civil service test for a job at the IRS, for they not only paid more but gave promotions often, sick leave, and yearly cost-of-living salary raises. One of my nieces' husbands had worked for fifteen years for civil service, so I asked him about the test, telling him that I planned to take it for a job there. He told me I would be wasting my time, for they were only hiring veterans and college graduates. Even a niece, not his wife, told my sister that she felt sorry for me, for I didn't stand a chance of getting employment at the IRS.

I didn't let them discourage me, for I knew

my God would answer my prayers and help me get the job. I'd always been a good student in English, but math was my problem, especially fractions. I'd heard the test was composed of English and math problems.

I prayed about the test and God showed me in a dream a large blackboard filled with solved fraction problems. When I took the test, the English problems were easy, but when I came to the math part, I panicked, for it was a big sheet of fractions. Then I looked up from the test paper and saw the same large blackboard God had shown me in the dream. It had all the fraction problems on the test! All I had to do was copy them from the blackboard and fervently thank the Lord. In a few weeks, I was called for an interview and got the job. I started to work the next week. Our Lord is so good to us when we trust him!

I really enjoyed working there and made several good friends. I worked there until I retired and had several promotions and pay raises, besides getting a half-day vacation and half-day sick leave every payday. I'd let my off time accumulate until I could have a good vacation. It was interesting, and I learned a lot about our government and the laws of the land. For example,

I learned how to write a will and wrote several for the family and friends. I learned that without a will, if you have real estate, the government can make you pay an inheritance tax that is sometimes so much the heirs can't pay it and the government gets the property. This caused several relatives and friends to have a will made for their protection.

When I look back over my life, I realize how my Lord has always guided, protected, and prepared me for what was ahead. The brief nurse training prepared me to take better care of my children when they were ill, and the government job helped not only me but several relatives and friends know the importance of having a will.

Ken Dies and Rosalind Is Supernaturally Healed

Before Ken married, he told me that God had let him know he would not live to see his thirty-fourth birthday but would have a short ministry. After his death, his wife told me he had told her the same thing. When he drowned just before Christmas in 1973, I was grieved but not surprised. I'll always miss him but know that he is with God. I've never wept for him, for I thank God for extending his life even more than I asked.

I'd always loved his wife, Esther, and had never seen their little girl. I wanted very much to see them both. I wrote Esther, asking her to come see me in Memphis and bring her little daughter, that I would be glad to pay for their trip. She soon came for a short visit, for she had a real estate company and couldn't be away very long. She wouldn't let me pay for the trip and even rented a car so we could go places together.

It was great to see her and my granddaughter, and we had a wonderful visit.

Since then I've visited them in Arizona, and they have been back to Memphis several times. Each Thanksgiving for many years she has sent me a round-trip plane ticket to spend a week with them and takes off work for us to be together.

After Rosalind got divorced, her ex-husband remarried so that he could get custody of their children, but he soon put them in foster homes. Five years later, Rosalind married a man who promised to help her get her children back. His family members were highly respected business-people and had a lot of influence in their town not far from Memphis. They had built a nice parsonage for their pastor and given it and the land to their church.

I thought their son was like them but was wrong. He did get her little daughter from the second foster home her dad had placed her in after he took the children from Rosalind. Her new husband was fairly good to the child until they had a baby girl, whom he spoiled and made

Rosalind's daughter give up everything for, even a stick she was playing with. He beat her unmercifully over the smallest thing. When Rosalind tried to help her daughter, he would abuse her too.

He started drinking heavily and beating her almost every night. She tried to leave him several times, but he'd always promise to do better. He did buy them a nice home, but Rosalind couldn't enjoy it for his cruelty. When she wouldn't stop going to church and talking about the Lord, he left her for another woman, got a divorce, and moved in with this woman.

When he left Rosalind, he told her he wouldn't pay child support or alimony and that he was going to sell the house. He did sell it, but I had the faith to put my hands on the real estate sign that said "Sold" and rebuked the sale. In a week's time, the sale fell through, and he had to return the earnest money he'd been given.

I helped Rosalind get a good lawyer who helped her get child support until their daughter was eighteen (she was only six then) and alimony for Rosalind for two years, after her husband had said he'd never do anything for her and their daughter. He just didn't know the power of God and prayer! Rosalind got half the sale of the home when it was sold years later. She bought a mobile home with most of it. She cared for several children for an income.

I had to stay with her most of the time until her younger daughter, Jennifer, was in high school. During this time, Rosalind got a bad infection from surgery. The doctor gave her three kinds of antibiotics, but they didn't help. Her body became swollen. He inserted tubes on both sides of her body to drain the infection, but it only got worse. Then her skin burst, and heavy fluid flew out and hit the wall. The infection turned to gangrene, and but for the grace of God and fervent prayer, she would have died. The gangrene infection lasted three months, and people usually die in two weeks or less. Finally the Lord healed her, and I can never thank him enough!

A few years after she was healed and was still taking care of children, she met a really nice man through the local cab company. She had called the cab for a doctor's appointment, and I answered the door when he arrived and told him to wait a few minutes. Then I told Rosalind, who wasn't quite ready.

Later, he said he thought I was his customer, and when Rosalind came to his cab, he thought,

Wow, she's gorgeous! He asked her if she was single, and when she said yes, he wanted her phone number. They started dating and were married on New Year's Eve.

I'd prayed for years for God to send a good Christian man for a helpmate to Rosalind. Bobby was the answer. At last my daughter had someone decent and loving to make a home with. How I thank the Lord for finally giving her a good life!

After Many Trials, Vern is Blessed

Vern did all he could to make a good home and marriage with Claire, but she was never satisfied. He made an excellent salary and bought her a lovely brick home in Boise, a baby grand piano, a sports car, and even a double-size mobile home like she wanted to be near her parents on the Newness of Life ranch. After ten years of marriage and two dear sons, she divorced him for a man with whom she was working.

He was so brokenhearted he didn't want to live. He asked me if I'd come to Idaho to care for his two boys so he could have them. I agreed but told him I'd have to give up my job at IRS and he would have to support me. Then he told me that Claire had not been paying the house notes as he'd thought, for he gave her his check each week to pay all the bills and use the remainder as she pleased. He said he was about to lose the house.

I asked him how far behind the notes were and sent the money plus an extra hundred dollars for him. This helped him keep the house and buy some badly needed tires for his Datsun truck. We decided it was better for me to keep my job, for he wasn't sure he could get the children.

One night after work, I called him and let the phone ring for at least five minutes. I felt sure he was there and too miserable to answer the phone. At last he answered it, and I was able to encourage him to have more faith and hope for the future. Later he told me that he'd been sitting with a pistol in his mouth, trying to get the courage to pull the trigger. Thank God for having me call and stay on the phone until he finally answered it!

Not long after this, I was packed and ready to go to Golden, Mississippi, for a revival with a famous evangelist from Chicago. We were to leave at eight the next morning when I suddenly felt that I should stay home. I did not know why then but felt the urgency to stay home, even though I'd looked forward to this revival for weeks. When my friend called to say she was on the way to pick me up, I had to tell her I couldn't go, even though my luggage was packed. She couldn't understand but went without me.

A couple of hours later, I received a long-distance phone call from Vern's mother-in-law in Boise. She said she'd just put Vern on a plane for Memphis, and he would arrive at one o'clock. Then I knew why God had kept me from leaving home for the revival. Claire was getting married that day, and it would have been too hard for Vern. Thank you, Lord, for keeping me home.

Soon Vern got a job at St. Francis Hospital in Memphis in the radiology department but was very unhappy over losing his family. He told me to never pray for him to marry again, that he had been a failure. I told him it was not his fault; he'd just been too good to her and spoiled her.

Without telling him, I began praying for God to bring a sweet Christian woman into his life and give him peace and a good life again. Three years later God answered this prayer too.

I had given Vern several good Christian books to read, but he wasn't interested until I gave him *I Believe in Visions* by Kenneth Hagin of Tulsa, Oklahoma. This was the life story of Brother Hagin, telling of God's great healing and delivering power in his life. This book caused

Vern to want to go to Tulsa, where Brother Hagin had a church and Bible college. He called a hospital there and made an appointment for an interview for employment in their radiology department.

One of the members of the church Vern was attending in Memphis had a sister in Tulsa who was a schoolteacher. She gave Vern her sister's phone number to contact her if he needed any information about churches and housing in Tulsa. After they met, they started dating and were married the next year. When I met her at Christmas before they were married the next June, I knew she was the one I'd been praying for God to send Vern to share life with.

She is a wonderful Christian woman with lots of love and wisdom, and is a precious help-mate for my son. She is also a dear daughter-in-law but is more like a special daughter to me. They have a beautiful home in Tulsa, and they have been married over twenty-five years. What a good God we serve!

Vern's sons are now married and have children. Vern and his wife, Mary, keep in touch and have visited them several times. They have four grandsons and two granddaughters. The boys love Mary, and so do their wives and children.

They now appreciate and love their dad, and he is happy to be reunited with them after so many years. God is good!

More Changes

A few months after retiring from the IRS, I heard about some new apartments being built for low-income recipients. I certainly qualified since I had only my social security check now.

I went to check on them, and even though they were only one-bedroom apartments, they were nice and in a good neighborhood. I rented one and soon moved in. I had to give my den furniture, extra bedroom suite, and breakfast set to relatives and friends, but I still kept more than I needed, especially books. I had a large bookcase in my living room and one in my bedroom, for I love to read.

This move took place about a year before Rosalind's second husband left her and gave their little daughter to his parents. It took a lawyer and much prayer for us to get the child back. Rosalind got custody on the condition that I stay with the child while she worked, so I could go back to my home only on weekends

I had to ride the local bus each week unless a

friend of Rosalind's came for me. After a while, I decided to find an apartment nearer her, but as I was praying one day, I heard the words "Stay where you are; I shall use you there." I was startled but knew that it was the Holy Spirit telling me what to do. I lived in that apartment for thirty-two years.

Soon after that, we had a new pastor take our church, which was only a block from me. He had not been there long before he wanted me to start teaching a class for young adults. He told me that he'd order literature for me to teach, but I asked him if I could teach from the Bible and let the Holy Spirit guide me. He liked that idea and agreed.

Each week I'd pray for God to give me a lesson that would help the young people. Soon the class members started bringing their friends and neighbors. One young woman brought twelve new members. They soon filled the room, and sometimes it was standing room only.

It's truly wonderful how our God blesses our efforts when we try to help others and let them know how very much God loves them and wants to meet every need. As I sought God's help to win these young adults to a greater revelation of his power and love, he began to bless me too and gave me a greater love for the Bible and understanding of peoples' needs.

One young man, who was an alcoholic, gave his life to Jesus and became a preacher. One young woman on drugs and having an affair with a married man turned to the Lord and is now a wonderful Christian. Another young married woman and her husband got on fire for God and soon received the gifts of the Spirit and became great witnesses for Jesus, as well as a wonderful influence in the church. It's amazing what God can do.

After several years, the pastor resigned, for two other pastors wanted to take over the church. The church had several pastors after that, but none of them lasted very long. Finally the church was sold to another group, and two friends and I started going to another good church not far from us.

I started teaching the adult Bible class at that church, and again I asked the Lord to direct me and use me to help others. He answered my prayer and has used me to teach anointed lessons.

We have a precious body of members in our church, both white and black, and we love one another and the Lord. The pastor and his wife are the most godly I've ever known, and I'm so very thankful for them. We truly have a scriptural church that reaches out to people, showing love and compassion to everyone and helping them whenever there is a need, either spiritual, financial, or physical. God's love is manifested among us, and there are no little cliques or special groups nor respecter of persons there. It is indeed the sweetest and best church I've been blessed to be a part of.

Some Unusual Experiences

After my mom died when I was a teenager, God gave me the gift of poetry, and I'd write poems as I was led by the Holy Spirit. I'd only write one or two a year until 1998, when God told me that he was anointing me to write his words and messages in poetry.

Since then it's amazing how our God has blessed and anointed me to write on any subject or person that I ask him to. I've had several poems published and have written a book of poems and miracle experiences. What a mighty God we serve!

In 1998 I became closely associated with a neighbor whom I'd lived near for over fifteen years. I had known him only as a good man always ready to help people. Then one day he asked if he could visit me while his air conditioner was being repaired. We talked a lot and got to know a lot about each other on that first visit.

He started visiting me every day, and we

talked a lot on the phone. He was so very understanding and had such a great sense of humor, as well as a beautiful voice for singing, that I began to enjoy being with him more than anyone I'd ever met. He also loved the Lord; we told each other wonderful experiences we'd had with the Lord and how much he had helped us in times of need.

Soon he asked if I would like for us to be together all the time, and we began to talk about marriage. I'd been single for over thirty years since my husband died and was enjoying life on my own. Over the years, I had turned down several marriage offers but was seriously considering it now.

Then one morning as I woke up feeling God's presence and started singing songs of praise and worshiping the Lord, I realized that I could not marry him and serve my God the way that I wanted to. I called and told him the way I felt, and he said that he loved the Lord too. But I told him he just didn't feel the deep love and presence of God that I felt, and he wouldn't understand or appreciate the way I worshiped him, sometimes even during the night.

We remained friends until he moved to Atlanta to be with his sons but never talked of marriage again. I thank the Lord for knowing him and the sweet times we spent together. I'd never known a man before who was so gentle and understanding yet lots of fun to be with. For the first and only time in my life, I felt free and happy in the presence of a man. Though I loved him, I don't regret not marrying him, for the peace and love of God comes first with me.

In May of 1998, as I was shopping at the mall, I started having chest pains and soon was very lightheaded and dizzy. I asked the Lord to take care of me then hurried to finish my shopping.

My next-door neighbor had become a wonderful Christian friend, and we spent lots of time together. She had told me to always let her know if I needed her for anything, so I called and told her about the chest pains. She said she'd be right over to take me to my doctor.

I had a few flower plants I hadn't finished transplanting the night before, so I hurried outside and put them in my flowerbed. She came over and said we'd better hurry, but I told her I needed a few minutes to change clothes. When I was ready, she said I shouldn't have done anything except hurried to the doctor. I laughed and said if it was my time to go I wanted to be clean! It's wonderful not to fear death but know God is with you.

The doctor sent me to the hospital, and they began taking X-rays, EKGs, and other tests. They found that I had a twisted artery in my chest, and they started giving me intravenous treatments and antibiotics to straighten it out.

The doctor was worried, for it was very serious and rare for a person to have a twisted artery. Even though I knew the danger, I wasn't worried and stayed cheerful and happy all the time in spite of all the X-rays, blood tests, EKGs, and other tests they kept doing. I even read some of the poems God had given me to some nurses who tried to help me by showing sympathy. Two poems they especially liked and asked to make copies of. One poem was titled "True Happiness."

True Happiness

Happiness is the joy of living,
Happiness is the love of giving,
Happiness is knowing the Lord.
To wake up in the morning with a smile on your face,
To throw your arms toward heaven and his love embrace,

Knowing Jesus loves you and has taken your place.
Oh! The wonder of walking with Jesus each day!
Of knowing he'll help you and show you the way.
No matter what danger or trials you face,
He'll always be there as your guide.
Though the world's in turmoil, God gives us peace.
His love shall sustain us, though dangers increase.
His power shall protect us through sunshine and rain
Until he comes back to earth again.

I was in the hospital for almost a week, but it seemed more like a vacation, for I felt the joy and assurance of the Lord intensely!

I'd had lots of visitors and flowers, as well as lots of phone calls. My good friend and neighbor called me a lot. One day he called me four times, for he was very worried about me. He just couldn't believe I was okay, for he didn't know God's love and power as I do.

When I went back to church, my pastor asked me to come up front and tell the people about the miracle healing I'd had. He told the people he'd hurried to the hospital and expected to find me moaning and groaning, but instead I was smiling and telling the nurses about God's power and love.

When I gave my testimony, I read the poem "True Happiness," which had meant so much to one nurse she had read it to several patients. She said one critical patient had been very encouraged and blessed from it and just couldn't believe that another patient had written it. Thank God for the gift of poetry to help others.

My pastor liked the poems God gave me and often asked me to read one to the church. When we had special occasions like Mother's Day and Easter, I was asked to write a poem for the event, and God always gave me one.

The last few months before the year 2000, much was being said about the dangers ahead, that computers would go out and many other bad things would happen. They named it Y2K, and many people were very upset about it. I asked the Lord to give me a poem about it, and he did. I read it to the church, and it was put in the church bulletin.

Y2K What It Means

Y2K, year 2000, what does it mean?
It means our Savior is now on the scene.

He's here to help you, so don't be afraid.
His words are being fulfilled; the plans are made.
The enemy would tell you disaster is ahead,
But you'll have peace and safety if by him you're led.
Just ask him to guide you, he'll show you the way
To help those around you who feel such dismay.
The time is so near for the end of this age.
Then his glory will fall on the heavenly stage.
We will reign with Jesus forevermore.
Our eyes have not seen the great blessings in store!

As always, God had everything under control. There were no great changes as so many people expected in the year 2000. Even the computers were not affected but operated as usual.

The Bible prophecies are being fulfilled rapidly now. The Scriptures foretold that men would kill people, thinking they were pleasing God. In 2001, the terrorists attacked the U.S.A. and killed thousands of people at the World Trade Center in New York, thinking they were pleasing their God Allah.

They thought they would destroy America by doing this terrible mass murder, but God gave us a new president who was a God-fearing Christian and who had the wisdom to unite our country by calling for a day of prayer. Since then many nonbelievers have turned their lives around and started living for Jesus.

A few weeks after this prophecy, I was thinking about it and asked God what I should write about. Suddenly he began bringing things that I had long forgotten to my mind. Then I knew I should write this book. When I think of the many, many times that he has protected me, delivered me, and healed me, I just can't find words adequate to express my gratitude and love for him.

My Miracle Healing

Satan has tried to destroy me and my love for God by bringing more trials and near death experiences than I've ever had in one year. Three times this year I've been in the hospital, had two emergency surgeries—hip replacement and cancer—and had fluid on my lungs.

Instead of turning from God and blaming him, it has made me appreciate him more, for I know I would not be alive without God's miracle healing! These experiences and surgeries have opened doors for me to testify of God's great love and healing power. Like Paul in the Bible, I thank the Lord for using me to help others know how great our God is and how much he loves us.

I was so shocked at first when the nurses at the hospital were so rude and actually cruel after hip surgery, for always before the nurses had been so helpful and kind to me. This time they even kept the water and signal button for their help out of reach. I had to lie in pain, thirsty and helpless except for the Lord. I finally realized I had to pray for them, for they were being used of the devil to come against me.

After I began praying for them, staying cheerful and friendly, they began helping me as they should. When Rosalind had come to the hospital to see me and saw they neglected to help me, she offered to stay at night, but I wouldn't let her when I knew she needed to be there for her husband. Sometimes our tests come in unexpected ways.

A few days after cancer surgery, bad complications set up, and I had to see the doctor again. He told me the cancer was malignant, and the tumor had doubled its size while I was waiting for my hip to heal enough for another major surgery. I didn't have long to live. He said all of us have a time to die, and my time had come.

I told him God could heal me of malignant cancer and he would. The doctor said that God's will had to be done; then I told him it was not God's will to take someone who loved him and was doing all she could to help people. Besides that, I still had prayers to be answered and things to do, and I was going to live to see this happen. He just looked at me sadly.

The next time I went for a final checkup, the

doctor told me I was free of cancer. I just smiled and said, "That's answer to prayer." He agreed to that but told me I needed to take radiation treatments so the cancer wouldn't return. I refused, for I knew God had healed me permanently. He gives abundant life!

My journey with God has been very interesting and sometimes exciting. Our Lord is still showing me more of himself and how truly loving and powerful he is! As the Bible says, "No mere man has ever seen, heard, or imagined what wonderful things God has ready for those who love the Lord" (1 Corinthians 2:9 TLB). Then it goes on to say that he reveals them to those by his Spirit.

The Lord has been so real and precious to me this year and gave me so many miracles! The doctors thought I'd be paralyzed and never walk again after hip surgery and that I'd soon die after cancer surgery, but I'm free of cancer and walking again! I'm enjoying a free and happy life more abundantly than ever. I often sing the song, "My God is real, real in my soul. I know he's real for he has healed and made me whole. My love for him is like pure gold, for he is real and I can feel him deep in my soul." God gave me the following poem that tells what Jesus means to me.

What Jesus Means to Me

Jesus, you're my help when I am weak,
My strength in times of need,
My peace, my joy, my everything.
Lord, you're my friend indeed!
When in doubt, you show me the way.
When in danger, you protect me from harm.
When lost or confused, your sweet name I use,
And you rescue me from all alarm!
When lonely, I find comfort in your precious word,
And feel your loving presence surround me.
Then I lift my voice in praise
And a standard you raise
So nothing on earth can confound me!

listen|imagine|view|experience

AUDIO BOOK DOWNLOAD INCLUDED WITH THIS BOOK!

In your hands you hold a complete digital entertainment package. Besides purchasing the paper version of this book, this book includes a free download of the audio version of this book. Simply use the code listed below when visiting our website. Once downloaded to your computer, you can listen to the book through your computer's speakers, burn it to an audio CD or save the file to your portable music device (such as Apple's popular iPod) and listen on the go!

How to get your free audio book digital download:

1. *Visit www.tatepublishing.com and click on the e|LIVE logo on the home page.*
2. *Enter the following coupon code:*
   3ff8-c38f-9889-ef22-54e8-aa0b-bb27-2853
3. *Download the audio book from your e|LIVE digital locker and begin enjoying your new digital entertainment package today!*